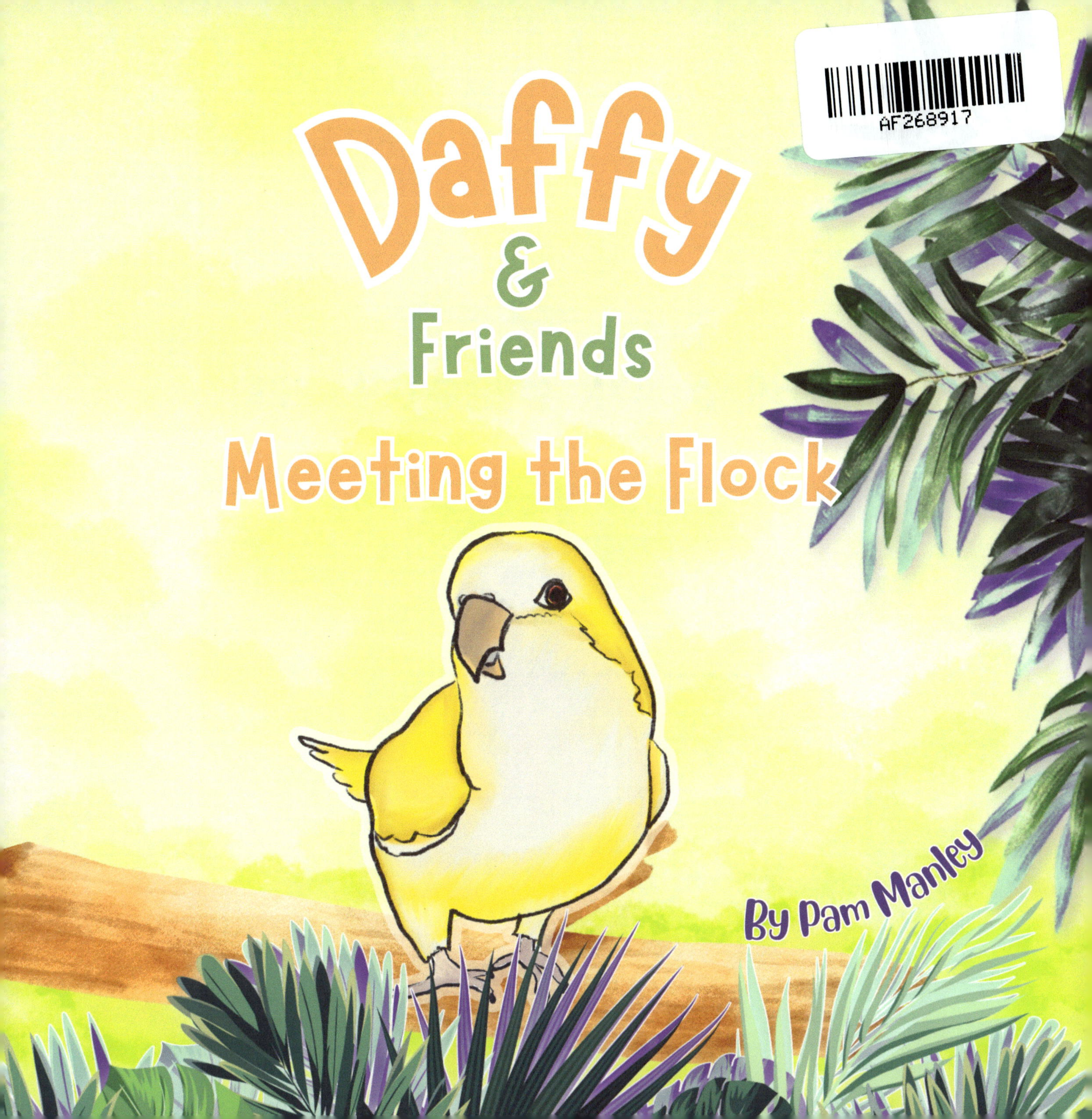

Daffy
& Friends
Meeting the Flock
By Pam Manley

This book belongs to:

NANA'S
ADVENTURE
BOOKS

Hello! I'm Daffy.

I'm a yellow Quaker parrot.

I can say many words.

I am very chatty

with my flock and my

mom.

I live in a big house with my mom and six other birds.
They are my flock and I enjoy spending time with them.

I have yellow feathers,
a pinkish beak, and dark red eyes.

I say good morning to my mom everyday.

My first word was
"Quack Quack",
so my mom named me
Daffy.

I can also sing Happy Birthday.
My mom thinks I'm very
talented and funny.

I want to introduce you to
my flock members.

This is Sunnie.

He is a yellow budgie and is the first member of the group.

He likes to eat seeds and fruits.

He likes to tell stories and jokes.
He is an active and playful budgie who always
attempts to boss everyone else around.

This is Stormy.

She's a light blue budgie.
She also loves Paulie.
She's very curious and playful.

She likes to eat millet and vegetables.
She likes to fly and explore, and she
always finds new things to do.

She is very beautiful and proud,
but also loyal and loving.
She is very independent.

This is Blue.

She's a blue budgie,

who is the most adventurous

of the group.

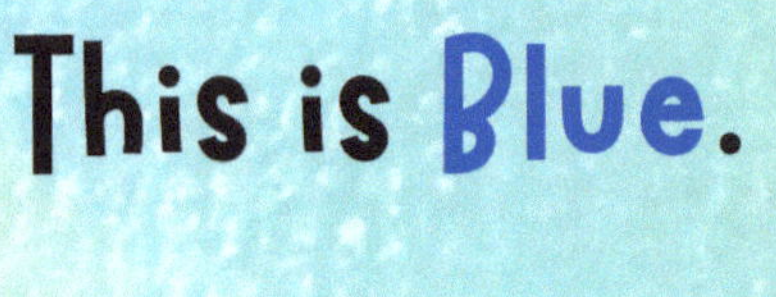

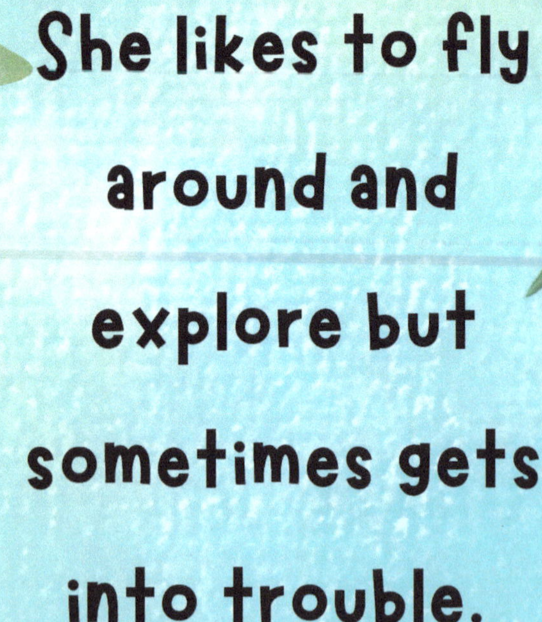

She likes to fly

around and

explore but

sometimes gets

into trouble.

She is not very talkative,
but she loves to whistle and sing.

She likes to eat pellets and sprouts.

She loves all the other flock members and is determined when she wants something.

She is also the youngest of the flock.

This is Mango.

He is a Sun Conure.
He is very bonded to our mom,
very bright and cheerful,
but also noisy.

He likes to sing and dance, and sometimes he annoys the other parrots with his loud voice.

He loves to show off his flying skills.

He loves to cuddle with our mom.

Mango is the oldest flock member.

This is Paulie.

He's a rose crown conure.
He is very playful and the clown
of the flock.

He likes to explore new
things and hang upside
down.

He is very quiet most of the time and only makes noises in the evening when he refuses to sleep.

He is a party parrot at night and tries to wake everyone up with all of his jokes.

He's very loyal and caring,
sweet and lovable.

He likes to eat pellets and corn.
Paulie loves music and dancing.

This is Clover.
She is a green quaker,
and she is my best friend.
She is very beautiful and amazing.

She is very sweet and smart.
She loves to play with her toys.

She likes to eat nuts and grapes.

She likes to cuddle and style my feathers.

She can also be very protective and jealous

at times when I play with my other friends.

We all live together in a
big house with our mom.

She's very nice and loving,
and she takes good care of us.

She feeds us, cleans our houses, plays
with us, and talks to us.

She gives us hugs
and kisses, and she
tells us stories.
She's the best
mom in the world.

We have a big room with a tree perch
that we play on daily.

It's our favourite place in the house.

It has branches, leaves, flowers,
and fruits.

It has swings, ropes, ladders, and hoops.

It has everything we need and want.

It's our favourite place.

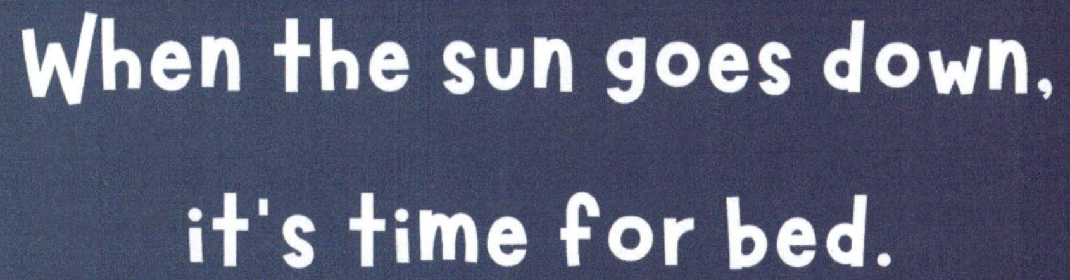

When the sun goes down,
it's time for bed.

We all go to our perches, and we say
goodnight to each other and to our mom.

We fluff our feathers,
close our eyes, and fall asleep.

But before we do,
I always sing a song.
It goes like this ....

Nighty night, nighty night,
Nighty night Little baby.
Nighty night, Nighty night,
It's time to go to bed.

Night Night Daffy,
Time For Bed.

Hope you enjoyed meeting
my flock members.
They are all very special and unique,
and I love them very much.

They are my family.